INTERACTIVE **WORKBOOK**

TRUE INTIMACY™

A Survivor's Guide to Restoration

Thank you to Brinda Carey for your contribution to *True Intimacy*.

BOOKLOGIX
Alpharetta, GA

The resources contained within this book are provided for informational purposes only and should not be used to replace the specialized training and professional judgment of a healthcare or mental healthcare professional. Angela's Voice and the publisher of this work cannot be held responsible for the use of the information provided. Always consult a licensed mental health professional before making any decision regarding treatment of yourself or others.

Copyright © 2013, 2023 by Angela's Voice

Second Edition

All rights reserved. No part of this book may be reproduced or transmitted in any form or by any means, electronic or mechanical, including photocopying, recording, or any information storage and retrieval system, without permission in writing from the author.

ISBN: 978-1-61005-979-4

This ISBN is the property of BookLogix for the express purpose of sales and distribution of this title. The content of this book is the property of the copyright holder only. BookLogix does not hold any ownership of the content of this book and is not liable in any way for the materials contained within. The views and opinions expressed in this book are the property of the Author/Copyright holder, and do not necessarily reflect those of BookLogix.

∞ This paper meets the requirements of ANSI/NISO Z39.48-1992 (Permanence of Paper)

Author, Angela Williams, MFP
Evaluation by Emory Rollins School of Public Health
Design and Illustration by Mark Sandlin
Design production by Felicia Kahn

042523

CONTENTS

What is Intimacy? ... 1
   The Seven Components of Intimacy ... 2
   Why Intimacy is Essential ... 5
   A Closer Look at Intimacy ... 6
The Devastating Effects of Child Sexual Abuse ... 8
   Sexual Anorexia ... 9
The Healing Process ... 10
   Sharing Your Story ... 11
      Listening Hints ... 12
   Accepting the Abuse and Assigning Responsibility ... 14
   Feeling and Dealing with Emotions ... 15
      Emotional Mastery ... 17
      Plutchik's Wheel of Emotions ... 17
   Learning New Ways of Coping ... 18
   Forgiveness ... 19
Key Intimate Relationships ... 20
   Intimacy with God ... 20
   Truly Loving Ourselves and Others ... 28
      Who Am I? ... 29
      Family and Others ... 30
      Developing a Healthy Romantic Connection ... 33
Intimacy with Our Spouse in a Sexual Relationship ... 34
   Physical Intimacy ... 35
   Flashbacks and Triggers ... 36
   Sensuality Exercise ... 39
   Sexual Attitudes ... 40
   Our True Intimacy Contract ... 42
Conclusion ... 43
Angela's Voice ... 44
Join the Angela's Voice Movement ... 46

Angela's Voice is a non-profit organization breaking the silence of child sexual abuse through awareness, prevention and healing programs. True Intimacy is one of a menu of programs designed specifically for adult survivors of child sexual abuse to aide in the healing process at the deepest level and in the most profound area of their lives: creating and sustaining intimate relationships. Those that love and support a survivor can also benefit by learning more about the struggles they face and solutions for recovery. The True Intimacy Interactive Workbook can be utilized independently, as a couple or in a group setting. We applaud your desire to learn more about the trauma of child sexual abuse, the crucial role intimacy plays in your life, and the path to healing.

WHAT IS INTIMACY?

What comes to mind when you hear the word "Intimacy"? Do you immediately think about a sexual encounter? Do you feel anxiety? Are you thinking "I want it, but it terrifies me?" Do you believe that it is something that you will never experience or that it only happens for other people? While most of us would agree we want or need intimacy, very few people understand what it is or how to achieve it. This workbook, True Intimacy, will help you gain a deeper understanding of intimacy and the important role it plays in your life.

Merriam-Webster's Learner's Dictionary has a very simple way of defining intimacy. It states that intimacy is "an intimate quality or state such as emotional warmth and closeness, the intimacy of old friends, the intimacy of their relationship; a quality that suggests informal warmth or closeness; sexual/physical intimacy or something that is very personal and private." As we move through this workbook, we will add to this definition painting a more definitive picture.

One of the most important aspects of this definition is the reality that intimacy is not just sexual – but intellectual, emotional, physical and spiritual. Intimacy is not defined solely by our relationships with our spouse, girlfriend or boyfriend, but can be with anyone with whom we choose to develop a close relationship, such as our children, parents or friends.

Intimacy also exists within our own souls as we confront or face truths about ourselves and learn to understand, love, and trust ourselves on a deeper level. This is also true concerning our relationship with God.

With these truths in mind, we can now define intimacy **"as that close interpersonal relationship with others that involves a spiritual, intellectual, physical and/or emotional connection in which we can be comfortable and even vulnerable with others and ourselves."**

THE SEVEN COMPONENTS OF INTIMACY

For any relationship to develop into a firm, long lasting, and truly intimate one, it must be based upon a mutual foundation consisting of seven key components:

TRUST: Trust is the most important and foundational element of a relationship and must be developed over time. We all have had someone hurt us by betraying that trust, each time making it harder to trust again. Trust means knowing that we can be ourselves without fear of condemnation, rejection or hurt.

As a person, we care about shows signs of integrity, we are able to slowly open up, allowing them closer to our true selves. Abuse creates emotional walls to keep people out and can destroy trust. Learning to trust can be much like taking down a wall one brick at a time. With each brick, we may keep one in hand, ready to start building the wall back. This is a natural response and in some ways healthy for our own safety; however, the effort to trust again is worth the struggle.

SAFETY: We develop strong and lasting intimate relationships with those that make us feel safe and secure. A person who makes us feel safe is someone whom we can turn to for comfort. We trust them not to willfully behave in a manner that will harm us physically, emotionally, or spiritually. When we find this safe haven with our soul mate, this relationship becomes a sanctuary, a place to escape the storms of life, and can represent a piece of heaven on Earth. Our safest relationship is with God who will never leave or forsake us.

"Be strong and of a good courage, fear not, nor be afraid of them: for the Lord thy God, he it is that doth go with thee; he will not fail thee, nor forsake thee." **Deuteronomy 31:6**

"My eyes are toward God in whom I take refuge…do not leave me defenseless." **Psalm 141:8**

RESPECT: Strong intimate relationships require the respect for yourself and others. Respectful behavior involves integrity, morality, goodness, and purity. These actions of reverence and respect contribute significantly to true intimacy.

COMPASSION: We find intimacy in the act of understanding issues from another's perspective. Others may only be able to sympathize, having not experienced the same pain. Yet, it is the willingness to put ourselves in the other's shoes that creates a level of intimacy. Selflessly caring about another's needs draws you closer. Intimacy grows when compassion and empathy play an important role in the relationship.

SERVICE: When we love deeply, we need to act upon these needs. In order to meet those needs, we must listen attentively **and** respond in a loving manner. The best relationships are those where each person anticipates the other's needs and trust it will be reciprocated.

"A new commandment I give unto you, that ye love one another; as I have loved you, that ye also love one another." **John 13:34**

Christ taught by example and stressed that even He, the Son of Man did not come to be served but to serve. **Matthew 20:26-28**

TRANSPARENCY: Having the properties which allow light to pass through so that objects behind or beyond can be distinctly seen.

Transparency in a relationship means being honest about how we feel and what is on our heart. Again, that all important component of trust must be present to give us the courage to open up and be real about what we are thinking and feeling as well as voicing what we want and need from the relationship. By being transparent, we allow ourselves to be vulnerable to God and others.

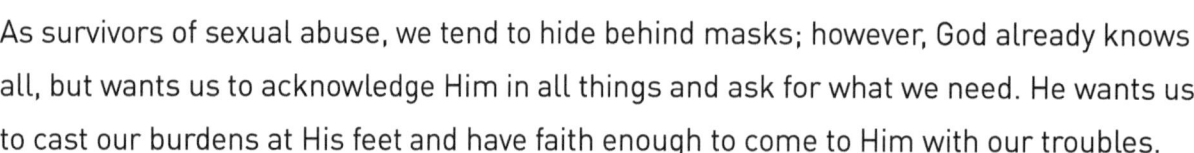

As survivors of sexual abuse, we tend to hide behind masks; however, God already knows all, but wants us to acknowledge Him in all things and ask for what we need. He wants us to cast our burdens at His feet and have faith enough to come to Him with our troubles.

"Lord, all my desire is before You; and my sighing is not hidden from You." **Psalm 38:9**

LOVE: "Your task is not to seek for love, but merely to seek and find all the barriers within yourself that you have built against it." **Rumi**

By attaining some level of intimacy through the previous six components, we grow to love the person with whom we are in a relationship. For some survivors, opening up to receive love is difficult as we must break down the walls of shame and worthlessness. A person in an intimate relationship with a survivor should understand these insecurities. The survivor may need to have their feelings validated repeatedly and be frequently reassured of your love and devotion.

Throughout the scriptures, you will find examples of the unconditional love of our Heavenly Father. You are His child and He longs for an eternal relationship with you. During your time of scripture study, read the verses listed under Love or Charity in the topical guide to understand the magnitude of His love.

"And now these three remain: faith, hope and love. But the greatest of these is love." **Corinthians 13:13**

WHY INTIMACY IS ESSENTIAL

Why is it important to talk about intimacy? Because the very nature of our humanity is built upon our ability to interact with one another and meet the very basic intricate needs of the soul: to be loved, to be useful, and to be accepted.

Yet, some child sexual abuse survivors live their whole lives void of intimate relationships. They withdraw from healthy hugs and comforting embraces. They are unable to openly and freely share their emotions. Many times, they equate intimacy with sex. The bottom line is this: without a proper, internal understanding of what intimacy is and what it might look like in healthy relationships, there will always be boundaries or stumbling blocks preventing the formation of healthy relationships, even the most intimate relationship of all – the one we are destined to have with God.

Intimacy plays a central role in the human experience because we have a universal need to be loved and accepted. We long for the security of knowing we are cherished, needed, and respected by someone. We long for physical touch: a pat on the back, a hug, a kiss, and passionate sexual experiences, which are all satisfied within intimate relationships. It is good and it is healthy to experience this beautiful, loving side of our being and existence.

Did you know that on a very foundational level, one of the very first ways a baby entering the world learns intimacy is through physical touch? Research around the end of WWII showed that orphaned infants, who were only touched for feedings and diaper changes, would eventually turn their heads away from people and die. The lack of intimacy literally killed them. Just because we grow up and mature doesn't mean that those needs go away.

Ask yourself one question: Am I dying a slow death from lack of intimacy? The following is a true testimony from a survivor who was experiencing a slow death in nearly every aspect of her life due to her lack of intimacy:

"When I was five, I was forced to participate in a sex act with my teenage siblings. Shortly thereafter, I was introduced to hardcore pornography and became fully indoctrinated into the incestuous patterns that had held my family hostage for generations. At 12, I was taken into relative foster care where the sexual abuse continued at the hands of other family members. At 15, after a brutal rape, I was placed in the foster care system where I remained until I aged out. As I matured into an adult, it was easy for me to express myself through rage, anger, laughter, rebellion, sex, achievement and ambition, but I lived a life fully detached from my own pain, shrouded in deep rooted secrecy, and drowning in shame. I didn't know how to talk about my feelings. I didn't know how to talk. Even in the midst of people, I felt completely alone – unable to connect. I didn't like being touched, hugged or anything unless it was with great force, rough or almost abusive. Any other kind of touch caused me great discomfort and unease. As a mother, I was a great provider and protector; but was unable to offer any emotional support or physical touch whatsoever to my young children. My husband, whom I had completely withdrawn from after the marriage, had to fill in the gaps. I was a mess and couldn't figure out how to fix myself. My family often told me that they felt like they lived with an ice queen, and didn't know how to reach me. I desperately wanted to love them, but didn't have the first clue how. My children learned to ask my permission before attempting to touch me in any way. I felt trapped inside my own body looking for a way out. The person my loved ones saw outwardly was drastically different from the person living on the inside of me – and she was slowly dying. As a result of my actions, even those who loved me were pulling away."

In the testimony above, you can see how this survivor struggled with intimacy issues on many levels. Her response to life as a survivor of child sexual abuse is, in fact, very similar to what other survivors might experience.

A CLOSER LOOK AT INTIMACY

The first intimate relationship a child has is with their parent(s) or other primary caregiver. They teach us through example that the world can be trusted to meet our needs, keep us secure and comfort us. As we saw from the example of the babies in WWII, the absence of these critical elements can be devastating - even terminal.

Because we are alive, we can assume we have received some level of intimacy. For survivors it has either not been enough or it has been invasive and damaging; therefore, we are lacking in the knowledge of how to build happy, wholesome relationships. The quality of the intimate care we received as children will affect the development of future relationships. As we grow older, we look to adults to learn if the world is safe and if we are worthwhile. The trust, or lack of trust, we have learned early in life is tested and refined. It is easy to see how sexual abuse by any one of these major influences would affect our ability to develop intimacy. Whether or not our parent(s) were aware, the child inside us feels abandoned, unworthy of protection and somehow damaged. The ability to develop and establish intimate relationships is hindered by these beliefs. Remember, even if a survivor is lucky enough to have had parents or caregivers who found out about the abuse and stepped up to protect them, the emotional belief of the child may have left an unhealthy pattern in their brain. It will take a great deal of work to restore a healthy belief system.

Just knowing the truth that we are loved and protected is not always enough, sometimes the damaging emotions are stronger. Child sexual abuse is a severe trauma that must be exposed, processed, and healed. Regardless of where the sexual abuse came from, each survivor begins to develop their own complex coping mechanisms in an attempt to appear "normal", to pretend nothing is wrong. Survivors of child sexual abuse begin to believe that if others knew the reality of who they are then they would lose any love and protection currently perceived in their lives. We come to believe that it is a necessity of life to hide who we really are. Apart from a healthy transparency how can we experience any level of intimacy?

THE DEVASTATING EFFECTS OF CHILD SEXUAL ABUSE

Survivors often think that they are the only ones experiencing the struggles they face from the devastating effects of child sexual abuse (CSA). Many times, they will say things like:

- I feel like I'm going crazy.
- I don't want to force my loved one to relive this nightmare with me.
- It was so long ago.
- I don't want to think about it.
- I don't think anyone would understand if I shared what was happening inside me.
- I just wish I was dead.

In reading through this next section, however, survivors will learn that many of these feelings are shared by all survivors of child sexual abuse.

Some of the debilitating effects caused by child sexual abuse may include, but are not limited to:

- ☐ anxiety
- ☐ fear
- ☐ anger
- ☐ depression
- ☐ suicidal thoughts
- ☐ re-victimization
- ☐ disassociation
- ☐ repressed emotions
- ☐ withdrawal
- ☐ promiscuity
- ☐ cutting
- ☐ self-hatred
- ☐ shame
- ☐ self-injury
- ☐ personality disorders
- ☐ frigidity
- ☐ chronic illness
- ☐ alcoholism
- ☐ sex addiction
- ☐ eating disorders
- ☐ insomnia
- ☐ PTSD
- ☐ drug abuse
- ☐ control issues
- ☐ co-dependency
- ☐ same sex attraction
- ☐ difficulty relating to others appropriately

The list of effects is long, and although some may not apply, those which do can be overwhelming; therefore, these effects need to be detailed and listed, giving survivors and those who love and support them an opportunity to grasp a full view of how the trauma from child sexual abuse might have manifested itself in his/her life.

EXERCISE:

Check the previous boxes of child sexual abuse effects that apply to you. Talk to your therapist to learn more about your aftereffects and what you can do to expedite healing.

Notes:_____
_____
_____
_____

SEXUAL ANOREXIA

Another difficulty for survivors is sexual anorexia. You are most likely familiar with anorexia as an eating disorder. The word anorexia comes from the Greek word orexis meaning without appetite. So Sexual Anorexia means without an appetite for sexual intimacy or the compulsive avoidance of sex. In an article written by Elizabeth Hartney entitled, "What is sexual anorexia?" sexual addiction expert, Dr. Patrick Carnes, is quoted as saying "sexual anorexics avoid sex in a variety of ways including:

- Persistent fear of intimacy, sexual contact, sexual pleasure, sexually transmitted diseases, etc.
- Preoccupation, to the point of obsession, with sexual matters, including the sexuality, sexual intentions, and sexual behaviors of others, and their own sexual adequacy.
- Negative, rigid, or judgmental attitudes about sex, body appearance, and sexual activity.
- Shame and self-loathing over sexual experiences.
- Self-destructive behavior in order to avoid, limit or stop sex. Those with sexual anorexia long for intimacy but believe that they do not deserve it or will not ever be safe in relationships so they impose a rigid sexual isolation on themselves. Like the eating disorder, sexual anorexics can binge and purge. They can go through cycles of total sexual deprivation followed by periods of promiscuity."

The point here is simple: The effects of child sexual abuse are real, and in some cases long term therapy may be necessary to help the survivor begin to lead a pain-free life. It is unrealistic for a survivor or their loved one to believe that they can simply get over the effects, regardless of the severity of the abuse.

NOTE TO SPOUSES AND LOVED ONES

Many survivors who have been sexually abused may not disclose their abuse, and if they do, they may not share the extent to which they have been abused. Those who love them and suspect that sexual abuse has taken place can educate themselves with the information shared here to gain better insight concerning how to relate to the survivor and aid in the healing process.

THE HEALING PROCESS

Healing comes for the survivor of child sexual abuse through these basic steps:

- ▶ Sharing your story
- ▶ Accepting the abuse and assigning responsibility
- ▶ Feeling and dealing with emotions
- ▶ Learning new ways of coping
- ▶ Forgiveness

These steps can look different for each survivor and his or her loved ones. Let's look at these steps and help you get started.

SHARING YOUR STORY

Revelations 12:11 says, they (the believers) have conquered him (Satan) by the blood of the Lamb and by the word of their testimony. Telling our "story" or testimony out loud is powerful. It changes people. Both the listener and the speaker change. Let's look at why the spoken word is so powerful. God created the world by speaking it into existence. God says that you are made in his image. You may never speak worlds into existence but your story spoken out loud to one other person will give you healing you cannot ever imagine. If you are the listener, don't fix, don't interrupt; just listen and validate. God will do the rest. Ask God for his strength and his power to find your voice or to listen with His heart.

There is healing and knowledge that come from speaking about our lives, pain and fears. Remember pain or sin can happen not only because of our own choices but also because someone else sins against us.

CSA is like that; an innocent child is coerced, forced or tricked into an unhealthy sexual relationship. The word "sin" in the Bible comes from the Old English archery term which means to miss the mark or fall short. This kind of sexual interaction falls short or misses the mark that God has set for a healthy sexual relationship. The term is not about fault, just about missing what God has set as the healthy standard.

So how does God call us to heal when sin is in our lives, even sin we did not cause? God promises that when we bring these things into the light, He will make them clear to us **(Eph. 5:13; 1 Corinthians 4:5)**. How do we bring these things into the light? We talk about them. In **James 5:16**, God calls us to confess our sins (ones we have committed and ones others have committed against us) to one another. God does not tell us we have to tell the whole world; he calls us to start with one trustworthy person.

Who should that one person be? It can be a counselor or trusted friend. Some survivors would rather start by telling another survivor. Others feel like they want to talk with a friend or family member. If you choose a therapist; be sure that they have experience with CSA. If you are talking with another survivor, a friend or family member, share the following helpful hints with them to help ensure success.

LISTENING HINTS

- Remember very few humans, survivors or not, have ever really been heard. Listening to someone without judgment, fixing, or interrupting is a gift that can never be taken away.

- A survivor's brain is not broken; it is their heart. Telling them truth will not fix them, but make them feel more broken.

- Trying to fix someone before you listen is disrespectful. You need to know the whole story before you share insight or plans. You may be fixing what is not broken if you have not listened. Remember there is a time for everything, and listening must come first!

- Tell them, "I believe you." An adult survivor fears that people do not believe the sexual abuse occurred. This is because they've been told by others that the abuse was all in his or her head, or the perpetrator told them no one would believe them.

- Keep your focus on what you are being told; resist the temptation to think about what you want to say. When you think about what you want to say, you have stopped listening. You will miss a great opportunity to show love by giving them your full attention.

- Do not interrupt to ask questions out of curiosity. These are questions that have nothing to do with the story. Examples: What was your dog's name? What city did you live in? What were you wearing?

- Avoid "Why" questions as they tend to express judgment. Why didn't you... The survivor wants/needs to be heard, not judged.

- Validate their feelings, even if you do not agree with all the details. They may say that something happened on Tuesday and you know it was Wednesday; it does not really matter. But, having someone say, "that must have been hard" or "You sound like you felt abandoned" will tell them you are listening and have heard their heart.

- Avoid the words 'should' and 'need to'. These are fixing and controlling words, not listening words. Your job is to listen.

Let's take a last look at **James 5:16**. Not only does God call us to confess or tell others about the sin in our lives, He tells us what to do after we tell or listen. **"Pray for one another so that you may be healed."** Notice God uses the word "healed". God knows that our hearts are broken, and we need Him to make them whole so we can love ourselves, Him, and other people.

SAFE LISTENING EXERCISE:

- You and your partner each pick something that makes you unhappy or uncomfortable but is small and not really important. They should have nothing to do with abuse, and hopefully are not too full of emotion i.e.: When you walk out of the room while I am talking, I feel like you aren't listening or don't care what I have to say.
- One person starts by telling how they feel in the situation they chose. Use only I statements in the following format: "When you____..., I feel____..."
- Avoid the temptation to place motive or blame in your statement. Speak only about how you feel. Keep it short, two to five minutes.
- When the talker is done the listener reports back what they heard. You said, "When I____...., You feel____...". If the listener is correct about the feelings, thank them for listening — tell them how good it felt to be heard.
- If they missed something important, thank them for hearing the parts that were right and then remind them of what they missed. You are not looking for an apology or a solution — this is an exercise in listening only!
- The listener then says what they heard again, adding what the talker told them they missed. Remember to thank your partner; listening correctly is a hard skill most of us have never learned.
- Switch roles.

When you get good at listening to the little things, you can move onto the bigger things. This exercise can help both the listener and the talker be ready for a full disclosure of CSA.

ACCEPTING THE ABUSE AND ASSIGNING RESPONSIBILITY

Believe that your experience happened and assign appropriate responsibility. This means fully understanding that you did nothing wrong. It means to release the blame for what has happened to you back to the perpetrator alone.

Twice in the Bible **(Matthew 18:6 and Mark 9:42)** it says that if anyone causes one of these little ones to stumble, it would be better for them to have a large millstone hung around his neck and to be drowned in the depths of the sea. Regardless of what anyone says, no child is emotionally prepared or competent to make decisions about sexuality. Sexual relations are to occur between a husband and a wife for procreation and pleasure. An adult that asks for or forces a sexual relationship on a child is wrong and is causing that little one to stumble and fall. God does not condone or approve of child sexual relations.

All adults that have sexual relationships with children have manipulated, violated, and coerced the child. They convince children that they will not be believed, or they cannot be forgiven for such bad behavior, or that if the child refuses or tells that their loved ones will be hurt or killed. Remember, children are vulnerable because they are still learning and they want to please others, be loved, be taken care of and protected. Sometimes the perpetrator uses gifts and attention to lure a child into their trap.

If your abuser was an older child, sibling, cousin, or friend, this does not change the facts: **You were a victim of someone else's sexual perversion.** They may have been a victim at one point, but when they abused you, they became the perpetrator. Talking about the abuse with a safe person, in a survivors group, and with a therapist can help you assign the appropriate responsibility for your abuse. Releasing the blame frees you to embrace truth, a critical component to intimacy.

NOTE TO SPOUSES AND LOVED ONES

Survivors are terrified of not being believed and this makes placing the appropriate responsibility on the perpetrator very difficult. Remember when someone shares this kind of pain with us we are walking on Holy Ground. Pray for God to help you listen and thank them for trusting you. Think before you speak so you will not make thoughtless comments that will hurt the survivor. Comments like: "Wow, I would never have guessed he would do that" cannot be taken back.

"Set a guard over my mouth, LORD; keep watch over the door of my lips." Psalm 141:3

NOTE TO SURVIVORS: Please remember your spouse is not your abuser. (If they are your abuser, get professional help). Remember to put the blame where it belongs. It will take time and practice to trust. Fervent prayer is always rewarded.

FEELING AND DEALING WITH EMOTIONS

In an article published through the Massachusetts Jane Doe, Inc. program, "researchers suggest that repetitive childhood sexual abuse significantly affects survivors' capacity to change or regulate their emotional states. In particular, the changes in the brain caused by trauma profoundly affect the survivors' capacities to soothe themselves" (Jane Doe, Inc. 2012).

Please know, however, that everyone is different in the internalization of trauma. As a result of the effects of child sexual abuse, many survivors will continue to exhibit elements of their trauma in nearly every relationship in their lives, whether they choose to live in secrecy, remaining silent due to their shame, pain, and/or denial; or whether they live very controlled lives, structuring everything and everyone around them. The outward expression of this hidden trauma is vast and wide.

We all have emotions. Some we have tried to deny and bury, but emotions are a gift from God. You may ask; why would a loving God want me to feel like this? Our God has emotions; the Bible says He is jealous, vengeful, that He cries over us, and longs to wrap us in his arms. We have been made in His image, so it makes sense that we have emotions too.

For God, emotions are neither good nor bad; they just are. People have labeled them as good or bad.

We think of pain as bad, but the pain from touching a hot stove tells us to move away and not do it again. Let's think of emotions as "feel good" or "feel bad". If you feel bad because you feel rejected, that gives you information. When you feel good after receiving a compliment, that gives you information. In order to not allow your emotions to rule your life, you must learn to use them to get information and learn.

For example, if you are excluded from a group, you may feel rejected. The rejection tells you this may not be a good place to build relationships. When someone compliments your work, they might be open to discussing a promotion--the good feelings told you that. But feelings can lie and we need to use them as a warning or a signal to look closer and think about our actions and reactions. It is possible that you have never allowed yourself to be a part of a group because you were afraid of what they would think of you, so the rejection you feel could be self-imposed. You might decide to become better acquainted with one person in the group and build up to joining in group activities. The emotions you felt were helpful in reminding you to go slow and be successful.

NOTE TO SPOUSES AND LOVED ONES

If you are a close friend, spouse or other family member of a survivor and they have strong emotions, what do you do? Give them a minute to calm down. Listen to them, really listen, and then validate them. We are not asking you to agree with every feeling or emotion they have; after all, we just noted that emotions can lie to us. But you can validate them by saying things like:

- That must be hard for you.
- You must have felt unprotected and scared.
- That would overwhelm me too.

EMOTIONAL MASTERY

CSA survivors have experienced a loss of innocence and trust. And when we start really looking at our lives, there are a host of other losses too. Grieving is needed and it takes time. There is no set timeline in which to accomplish this, but the process must start.

Isolation is one of Satan's favorite tools. Very little healing can happen all alone. It's okay to spend some time alone with God and your thoughts, but don't stay there. God wants us in relationships with others. Although others can hurt us, they can also strengthen, guide and encourage us. There is a child within each survivor that needs to be protected and comforted. It is only with other people that we can help that child within learn to trust and experience protection and comfort.

For many survivors naming their emotions is a huge problem. They have buried and denied them for so long that they feel numb or don't know what it is they are feeling. Naming our emotions allows us to begin dealing with them appropriately.

PLUTCHIK'S WHEEL OF EMOTION

Robert Plutchik, PhD created the emotion wheel, which has been improved upon multiple times since published in Emotion: Theory, Research, and Experience: Vol. 1. Theories of Emotion. You may find it helpful in labeling your emotions.

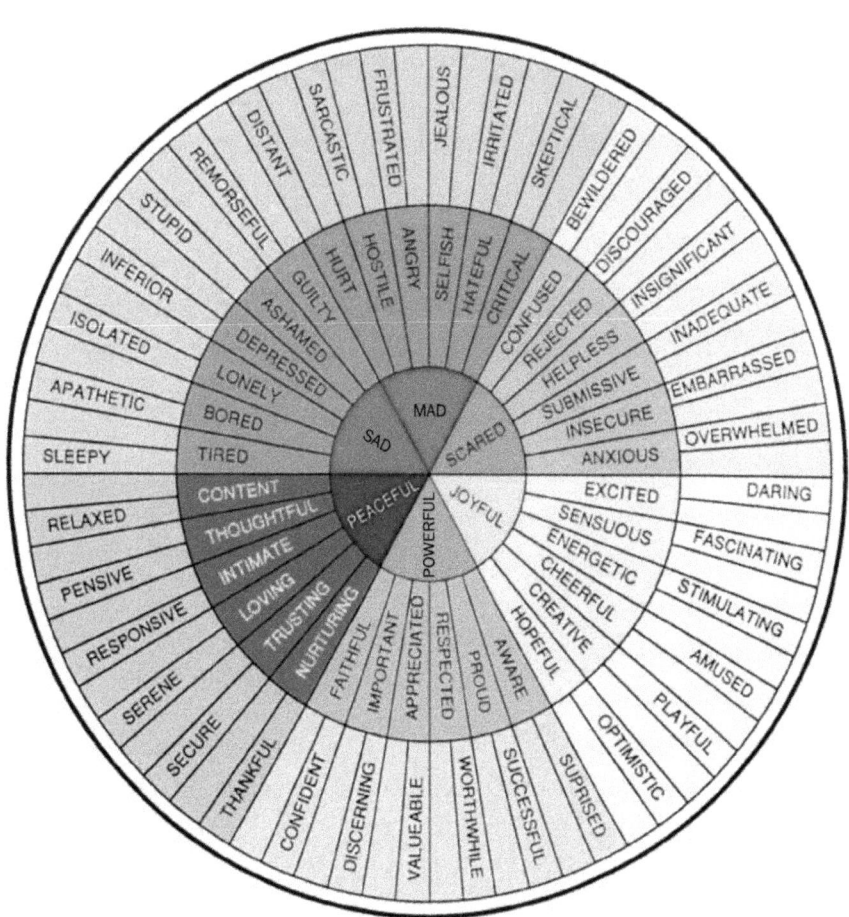

When a situation arises that makes you feel something but you are unsure what, go to the center of the wheel and identify which of the emotions is closest to what you are experiencing.

For example: Let's say you are in the middle of something and your spouse calls to you from the other room, "Honey, come here." You suddenly feel "mad", but you don't know why or if that is even exactly what you are feeling. Go to the wheel and locate "mad" in the center of the wheel. Then start working out from that point in the pie wedge to the outer edge of the wheel. Think about the other emotions listed: "hostile", "hurtful", "angry" and "frustrated". You identify with "frustrated", realizing you were doing something and your spouse expects you to drop everything and come whenever they call. Now you have an emotion you can discuss and work through. You can think about other times you might have felt like this.

LEARNING NEW WAYS OF COPING

Healing may mean taking a few steps forward and one back. Even though you are taking baby steps, you will one day look over your shoulder and realize how far you have traveled down the road to recovery. Here are some simple steps you can take:

Attempt to engage in safe relationships. Meet someone for coffee or a bite to eat. This way you are not letting them into your private space, which can feel dangerous. Some people find it helpful to have a list of safe topics beforehand. Figure out what will make you feel safe and comfortable and take this first step towards getting to know someone better. Join a support group. We all need a sense of belonging and survivors need other survivors. You need to be able to talk to people who understand what you have experienced. Try going to a support group. Don't worry if it takes several visits to speak; count showing up as a victory! If you don't have a group in your area, find an online forum that you can join. Be sure that they have the same values you do and that their guidelines make you feel comfortable before you invest emotionally. Remember that a live group will better meet your needs to connect on a more intimate level.

Seek therapy. An experienced therapist can help you process your emotions. Begin with individual therapy, then couple's therapy, if applicable. Therapists can help identify the areas where you are stuck, give you exercises that help build your emotional maturity, and meet your individual needs. Therapy should be a safe place to start practicing trust.

FORGIVENESS

"For all have sinned and fall short of the glory of God." Romans 3:23

God has given each person free will – meaning we have the ability to make our own choices and decisions. We will not go into the theological debate about free will here, but let us agree that the sins and bad choices of others sometimes cause pain for us. Sometimes the pain inflicted is unintentional. Other times, as in the case of what we endured as a child, the pain is specific and intentional.

For survivors of CSA, the very word "forgiveness" causes a vast array of thoughts and emotions, walls are put up, and we may even feel that our suffering has been invalidated at the mere thought of forgiving our perpetrator(s).

We should strive to understand that we live our lives in a fallen world. This means that the world is not free of sin as it was in the beginning when God created it. When Adam and Eve decided not to listen to God and were sent out of the Garden of Eden due to their disobedience, the protection they had while in the garden was taken. For this reason, bad things happen: people get old and sick, earthquakes, fires, floods and other disasters happen, and people, including us, make bad choices that hurt others.

"Do not judge, and you will not be judged. Do not condemn, and you will not be condemned. Forgive, and you will be forgiven." Luke 6:37 (NIV)

We are commanded to forgive; however, we are not expected to forget. Forgiveness doesn't mean we condone the hurtful actions nor should we put ourselves in harm's way again. It does mean that we have placed the burden at the Lord's feet and trust Him to provide justice for us.

"To forgive is to set a prisoner free and discover that the prisoner was you." Lewis B. Smedes

You don't need to understand why someone did the things they did in order to forgive. Child sexual abuse is a deep wound for which forgiveness will be a process. Along this journey to forgiveness, you will gain glimpses of understanding and greater peace. Do not burden yourself with guilt for the anger or struggle you face when it comes to forgiveness. Neither should you expect an apology from the abuser. You forgive to honor God and yourself...not them.

KEY INTIMATE RELATIONSHIPS

In this section, we will take a closer look at the key intimate relationships in our lives: God, Self, Others, and our spouse.

INTIMACY WITH GOD

"Who have I in heaven but You? And there is none upon earth that I desire besides You." **Psalm 73:25**

Our most important relationship is the one we have with God. By nature, we innately long for a relationship with our creator, just as children want this from their earthly parents. We want to understand who we are, where we came from, and why we are here.

In Genesis, we see that Adam and Eve enjoyed a special and deep relationship with God. GOD was truly their Father - fulfilling their spiritual, physical and emotional needs. The symbolism of them standing confidently naked before GOD is the ultimate act of vulnerability. They were completely exposed with no feelings of shame or guilt. They were confident in their trust in Him, as well as one another, and had no doubt that they were accepted and loved completely.

Just as Satan manipulated and deceived Adam and Eve, causing them to hide themselves from God out of guilt and shame, the perpetrator has used the evil of sexual abuse to destroy our innocence and leave us with feelings of inadequacy, self-condemnation, shame and guilt. These feelings cause us to hide from God, yet there is a deep desire within the soul to reconcile with God; to restore that intimate relationship He had planned for us long before our birth.

So we see a picture of Adam & Eve's close and very personal relationship with God, communing in the Garden of Eden, no stress, no worries, with complete assurance that God was listening to every word they uttered, and in turn they audibly heard God's voice. Don't we all long for this type of relationship with God? Don't we all want to know without a doubt that God is intimately with us, that He cares, that He loves us and is listening? Do you struggle to have this kind of relationship with God?

How would you describe your relationship with God? _____
_____
_____
_____

WHO IS GOD?

Do you believe that God is good, God is love and God is sovereign? When we question God, we must focus on His character. We may find it difficult to trust in God when we question, "Where was God in my abuse? Why didn't He deliver me, protect me, or help me? Why did He let me suffer?"

We have to accept that God was grieved over our abuse and our abuse was caused by man's free will, not God. Though it may be difficult, we must accept **Romans 8:28**, "**All things work together for good for those who love God and are called according to His purpose.**" We have to accept that God did not cause our abuse but He will use our abuse to His glory.

This may take a conscious effort to separate Life from God. Life cause pain; God does not.

CAN I TRUST GOD?

> Common Issues for Survivors:
> Blame God
> Feel God has failed me
> Feel God is punishing me
> Feel God is distant
> Faulty Belief System about God

When we are wounded by someone we trust, our ability to trust is destroyed. We may want to trust, but we have been so wounded that we are not able to trust. Trust is a muscle; sometimes a muscle that is strained and injured again and again, but it has to be rehabilitated just as an injured muscle: worked, stretched and continually challenged.

Trust and faith go hand in hand. If you do not trust, you do not have faith that God is for you and not against you, faith that God sees you as pure and righteous no matter what perversion has violated your life. Often we don't trust the parental figures in our life which impacts our ability to trust God and His greatest characteristic, God the Father. Our perpetrator may have even used twisted renditions of the Bible of his or her own making to justify abusing us, further crippling our ability to trust God.

The truth found in God's word states that God the Father loves us unconditionally as His children. When we struggle to receive that unconditional love, we struggle to allow that love to flow through us to ourselves and others. Accept that God loves you unconditionally and learn to trust His true characteristics, one step and one day at a time.

TO TRUST GOD WE MUST BELIEVE:

- God is good
- God is sovereign
- God is love

"Trust ye in the Lord forever, for in the Lord Jehovah is everlasting strength." **Isaiah 26:4**

Read **Luke 22:39-44**. How do you feel about Christ having endured the pain and sins of the world with such agony that He sweated blood? Do you trust that He understands your pain and suffering? _____

_____

_____

_____

EXERCISE:

Look in the topical guide of the bible for scriptural references on trust in God and God's love. Write them down. _____

_____

_____

_____

CAN I CONNECT WITH GOD?

For many of us, we have spent a lifetime running from God; He has spent our lifetime chasing us. He is closer than you think. We do not seek a God we cannot find; God does not hide.

"Ask and you shall receive, knock and the door shall be opened." He replied, "Because you have so little faith. Truly I tell you, if you have faith as small as a mustard seed, you can say to this mountain, 'Move from here to there,' and it will move. Nothing will be impossible for you." Matthew 17:20

God desires to have a close and intimate relationship with you. He cannot achieve that relationship on His own; you must also yearn for a close and intimate relationship with Him. What does any relationship need? A relationship needs time, attention, trust and communication. It is time that you commit to God, then you will learn to trust Him more and more each day. In that close walk, intimacy is cultivated.

TIME WITH GOD/TIME TO HEAL:

> Read **Deuteronomy 30: 8-14**. Write your thoughts about this passage and promise.
>
> _____
> _____
> _____
> _____

The scriptures are living and can powerfully impact your daily life. We can build a closer relationship with God by studying the scriptures and communicating with Him through prayer. The Holy Spirit is there to guide and teach us what we need to learn from scripture. Take time daily to meditate and be receptive to the comfort and guidance of the Spirit.

"Seek the Lord and His strength, seek His face continually." 1 Chronicles 16:11

PRAISE HIM:

"Let the word of Christ dwell in you richly in all wisdom; teaching and admonishing one another in psalms and hymns and spiritual songs, singing with grace in your hearts to the Lord." Colossians 3: 16

Listening to uplifting music can calm the soul and open up our hearts to the Spirit. We can offer prayers of thanksgiving through song. It does not matter how well we sing, but rather the feelings sent forth from our soul.

In song and/or prayer, count your blessings with a spirit of gratitude, being mindful of all the blessings you see and acknowledge in your life, before asking for what you need. This will help you gain perspective and be mindful of His presence in your life.

Read **Ephesians 5: 18-20.** What does the phrase 'make a melody in your heart to the Lord' mean to you? _____
_____
_____
_____
_____

"By Him therefore let us offer the sacrifice of praise to God continually, that is, the fruit of our lips giving thanks to His name." **Hebrews 13:15**

COMMUNICATE:

God communicates with us through scripture and via the Holy Spirit. We communicate with Him through prayer and by our actions. In Romans Chapter 8, God assures us that there is no condemnation of those who are in Christ Jesus, and assures us of His intercession on our behalf. He promises the Spirit will bear witness to the truth that we are His children if we seek an answer through prayer. He will bless us immeasurably with His glory.

Read **Romans 8:24-28**. What does this mean to you? _____
_____
_____
_____
_____
_____

"It is a joy to Jesus when a person takes time to walk more intimately with Him. The bearing of fruit is always shown in scripture to be a visible result of an intimate relationship with Jesus Christ." Oswald Chambers

The truth of God's word says that God loved you so much that He sent Jesus Christ as the ultimate sacrifice to die on a cross for all our shortcomings, our sins, and all of our failures, so we could be in a right relationship with God. Jesus Christ ascended to heaven and sent the Holy Spirit to comfort, to lead, and to live within each of us who believe.

God created everything to grow. If we are not growing, we are dying. We can grow without fear of rejection, knowing we will be accepted just as we are, and grow closer to God by receiving His love, abundant grace, and mercy. He expects you to come just as you are, with all your doubts, fears, even anger. We serve a BIG God who made us, knows us intimately, and is able to receive all of our emotions, good and bad. As we grow closer to God, He will reveal how to process each of these emotions.

The more we know God, the deeper our desire for more intimacy in our relationship with Him.

Though it is sometimes easy to identify with our loss and pain, we are more than our circumstances. How we endure these injustices and learn from them matters most. Adversity comes to every living soul and yet faith in God and enduring to the end with the hope of eternal salvation takes us down the road to restoration. Growing in an intimate relationship with God allows each of us to give that pain over to God so that we can experience true physical, emotional, and spiritual healing. God's love can pierce any pain and free us from any and all residual bondage from the abuse.

You will truly find the peace that passes all understanding when you learn and accept the true character of God and can build a trusting and connected relationship with Him. As you do this, you will understand your identity in Christ on a more intimate level. God is waiting for you to cry out to Him.

EXERCISE:

Put an empty chair beside you and talk to God. Tell Him about your anger, disappointment, fears, struggles and your loss. Then tell Him exactly what you want. He is listening. Now sit quietly and listen to Him. Write down what you feel or hear.

_____
_____
_____
_____
_____
_____

What does God think about you? _____
_____
_____
_____
_____
_____

GOD also speaks to us through His Word. Open your bible to your favorite chapter and read a verse that speaks to your heart. Write the verse in the space below and take time to ponder its meaning. Why does it speak to your heart? _____
_____
_____
_____
_____
_____

EXERCISE:

TRULY LOVING OURSELVES & OTHERS

God created us to commune with others and commands us to love Him first and love others as ourselves. This greatest commandment is stated clearly in **Luke 10:27**:

"Love the Lord your God with all your heart and with all your soul and with all your strength and with all your mind;" and, "Love your neighbor as yourself."

Because we survivors have been deeply wounded, we often find it challenging to love ourselves, and thus it is difficult and sometimes impossible to love others. Child sexual abuse destroys our self-image, self-worth, self-dignity and self-confidence. We are so ashamed that often self-hatred overrules our logic. Many survivors turn to self-destructive patterns of addiction, cutting, eating disorders, or promiscuity as punishment. It begins a cycle of self-destruction that can take years to break. Because of the stigma of child sexual abuse, we as survivors may spend years trying to stop destructive behavior, but never realize the root of the pain. There is also collateral damage in relationships as a result of the self-hatred and self-destructive behaviors. It is impossible to respect others if you don't respect yourself. It is impossible to repress pain and not self-destruct, and when pain is expressed, often it is in an explosion of rage.

EXERCISE:

Write down how you feel about yourself._____

_____
_____
_____
_____

Write down any self-destructive behaviors present in your life. _____
_____
_____
_____

What collateral damage in relationships has the pain of child sexual abuse caused in your life?_____
_____
_____
_____

WHO AM I?

You are an unconditionally loved and accepted child of God. You were created for a relationship with God and for a special Kingdom purpose. There is no experience in your life that God can and will not use. God is also too efficient to make it all about you. You must be confident in who you are in Christ Jesus. As a survivor of child sexual abuse, confidence in anything often feels foreign, and receiving anything good feels questionable.

We must learn to become our own best friend, our own advocate, and stop the damaging thought patterns that may plague our minds. The self-talk that says, "I am no good. I am worthless. I am stupid. I am weak." are all destructive, and must be replaced with truth: "I am valuable. I am beautiful. I am strong. I am smart."

"For you created my inmost being; you knit me together in my mother's womb." Psalm 139:12-14

"And even the very hairs of your head are all numbered." **Matthew 10:30**

EXERCISE:

Look in a mirror. Repeat 10 positive statements about yourself and then tell yourself: "I LOVE YOU"

(Suggestion: write these "I am" statements on your mirror with soap or list them on an index card to keep in your wallet and repeat daily)

FAMILY AND OTHERS

When we learn to love ourselves, we can love others. Superficial relationships may be the norm in our society, but they certainly are not fulfilling. People are in our lives for a season, a reason, or a lifetime. People we are most drawn to are those with whom we develop a deeper intimate relationship. We are drawn to people by common interests, proximity and mutual relationships. Growing a friendship means truly listening, encouraging, and nurturing that relationship as a seed that is planted and needs tending.

Sometimes our most challenging relationships are those closest to us: our family. As a survivor, you may feel as though your family let you down as a child by not protecting you from the sexual abuse. You may even be facing denial by family members that your abuse happened. Even worse, your family may be protecting the predator. You may be harboring unresolved resentment. These feelings of resentment and disappointment must be processed and can be addressed in a number of ways.

How would you describe your intimate relationship with family and friends?_____
_____
_____
_____
_____

It is important for a survivor to learn to distinguish healthy relationships from unhealthy relationships. We don't choose our family, and just because we are related doesn't mean that we must strive to have an intimate relationship. However, for those we love, we should make every effort to develop more meaningful relationships. We may receive comfort and support from these relationships. But we may also feel burdened by family members because of disrespect and/or betrayal. This is where we must practice forgiveness, compassion and boundaries.

Establishing good boundaries in difficult relationships will allow us space to heal. There is a fine balance in enforcing healthy boundaries. We must protect our emotions and define for others acceptable and unacceptable behavior. It is okay to distance yourself from those who continue to cause you pain.

Communication is crucial. We must be willing to open ourselves up, even in the smallest of increments, to those whom we trust and desire to develop a closer relationship, and express how we are feeling with our words. An example could look like this, "Mom it really hurts me when you tell me what a happy child I was growing up. I feel that you ignore the pain of my abuse." Often it is difficult for a survivor to share honest emotions because we were silenced in our pain growing up. Many survivors never tell of sexual abuse until adulthood, so it very difficult to express our true emotions. Survivors suffer fear or vulnerability and a sense of inadequacy because of the inability to stop the abuse as a child. These fears have to be overcome by building healthy relationships with family and friends.

We must also accept responsibility for those we have wounded through our pain, rage, anger and self-destructive behaviors. This may require a great deal of vulnerability in asking for forgiveness. If they don't know, break your silence and tell them you have survived a very traumatic experience. As result of that pain, you may have made some very bad decisions that led to broken relationships. It is never too late to ask for forgiveness and seek reconciliation.

EXERCISE:

With whom do you have the most challenging relationship? _____
_____
_____
_____
_____

Write down how they have wounded you in the relationship? How will you share your feelings? _____
_____
_____
_____
_____

Read **John 15:1-17**

In **John 15:9**, Jesus says, "As the Father hath loved me, so have I loved you; continue ye in my love." What does this mean to you? _____
_____
_____
_____
_____

In John 15:12-14, Jesus says, "This is my commandment, that ye love one another, as I have loved you. Greater love hath no man than this, that a man lay down his life for his friends. Ye are my friends, if ye do whatsoever I command you." What does this mean to you? _____
_____
_____
_____

Write down whom you have wounded. How will you seek to repair that relationship? ___
_____
_____
_____

DEVELOPING A HEALTHY ROMANTIC CONNECTION

In the course of building relationships, each of us will at some point find ourselves romantically attracted to someone. As a survivor of sexual abuse, it is of utmost importance that we learn to differentiate sex and lust from love and romance. Intimacy is more than the physical act compelled by lust or romantic notions. Some survivors may have a distorted sense of boundaries or no boundaries at all. Others may have no respect for their bodies, or others, because of the sexual abuse. Be cognizant of your feelings and strive to understand the underlying causes of your thoughts and actions. The first step is to work on recovery and learn to love, respect, and value yourself enough to care about how you treat your mind and body.

This also applies to the person for whom you have romantic feelings. Learn to love and respect him or her, and care about how you treat him or her physically and emotionally. All of these aspects combined are necessary for true intimacy and a satisfying sexual relationship. Sex outside of marriage comes with feelings of shame, guilt, vulnerability, and resentment, which break the sacred, intimate relationship bonds set forth by God and can further damage the sense of worthlessness felt by the survivor.

"Watch and pray, that ye enter not into temptation: the spirit is indeed willing, but the flesh is weak."
Matthew 26:41

SUBCONSCIOUS VOWS

I will never _____

No one will ever _____

What are the lies, caused by the manipulations of your perpetrator, which have you making these vows? What are the realities? _____

_____

_____

_____

_____

It is important to share about your sexual abuse with the one to whom you are intimately connected. He or she will be an active partner in your recovery and healing. Sensitivity and awareness of the healing process will also be necessary. It takes a strong person with patience to love and nurture a survivor back to health. As a survivor, be very selective in your future mate because it is a lifetime journey.

INTIMACY WITH OUR SPOUSE IN A SEXUAL RELATIONSHIP

How would you describe your intimate relationship with your soul mate? _____

_____

_____

_____

Even in marriage, the sex act itself may leave the survivor feeling vulnerable, abused, or violated. They may feel shame, guilt, fear, or even anger and resentment towards their spouse if other aspects of intimacy are bypassed. A survivor may struggle with sexual addiction, perversion, or pornography stemming from the sexual abuse which he or she endured. It is important to be transparent about these issues, study them, and discuss them with a counselor. Rational thought may offer temporary comfort. Logic will help in the battle to overcome these negative feelings; however, emotions are not bound by logic and reason.

For a healthy sexual relationship, the survivor must have a spouse willing to work with him or her on the building blocks of true intimacy. Being married to a survivor means willingly putting oneself into the recovery process and knowing that this will require a committed involvement in the recovery of your spouse. The spouse should learn about the issues the partner struggles with and not take these struggles personally. Take your burdens, hopes, fears, and the desires of your hearts to God in prayer.

As a survivor, you should work at acknowledging your love for your spouse in healthy ways outside of triggering sexual behavior. As a spouse, you should realize that some acts of sex can and will trigger memories of the abuse. When that happens, prayer is a powerful tool to help resolve anxiety and feelings of inadequacy. As a survivor, you must realize that you have lived through a traumatic experience that is real and emotionally damaging.

It is normal to feel sensations, flashbacks, anxiety, and even fear. We must deal with these emotions as they come and not try to suppress them. It is important to ground yourself in the moment, reassure yourself that those memories are the past and that you are safe now. Reassure yourself that your spouse loves, respects and honors you.

One of the most challenging struggles is to describe to your mate what you are feeling. Openly and honestly sharing your emotions and deepest feelings can invite your mate into your healing process. It will increase compassion and understanding of the trauma you are processing. In turn, your trust and vulnerability will grow as you are assured that you are in a safe, loving, kind and caring relationship. Without this open communication, your mate is left feeling helpless, which can build walls in your relationship. Trust your mate enough to love you through this pain.

PHYSICAL INTIMACY

Physical intimacy is characterized by romantic or passionate love and attachment, or sexual activity. The term is also sometimes used euphemistically for a sexual relationship. Sex is a sacred gift from God that has been misused and distorted in the lives of those abused. This trauma may then be manifest in perversion, sexual addiction, promiscuity, identity confusion, emotional detachment, and an array of other struggles with physical intimacy.

How Do We Deal with Physical Intimacy in Light of Abuse?

- Be transformed by the renewing of our minds.
- Allow yourself to be vulnerable and trust again.
- Use your words to explain what you need.
- Men need affirmation; women need affection.
- Reject the spirit of abuse in your bedroom.
- Give what you need.

Which of these areas causes you the most anxiety right now? _____
_____
_____
_____

Have you discussed your feelings with anyone? Who? Has it helped? _____
_____
_____
_____
_____

If your spouse is with you now, give them what you are longing for: a hug, a kiss, a backrub, etc.

FLASHBACKS AND TRIGGERS

Survivors will experience flashbacks. For some, they can be debilitating in their severity.

*The following is a definition of flashbacks by the Virginia Sexual and Domestic Violence Action Alliance, 2006.

"Flashbacks are when memories of past traumas feel as if they are taking place in the current moment. Many survivors of sexual violence experience these emotional returns to the trauma, believing themselves to be back at the scene of the attack or abuse. Flashbacks are also a symptom of PTSD.

Flashbacks can be triggered by many stimuli, such as sensory or emotional feelings. It can sometimes feel as though flashbacks come from nowhere, making it difficult to distinguish between past and present. They can often leave the survivor feeling anxious, scared, powerless, or any other emotions they felt at the time of their assault."

*"Anxiety Issues," National Institute of Mental Health, November 2, 2010

According to the National Institute of Mental Health, "Flashbacks may consist of images, sounds, smells, or feelings, and are often triggered by ordinary occurrences, such as a door slamming or a car backfiring on the street. A person having a flashback may lose touch with reality and believe that the traumatic incident is happening all over again.

Some flashbacks are mild and brief, a passing moment, while others may be powerful and last a long time. Many times the individual does not even realize that s/he is having a flashback and may feel faint or dissociate."

SELF-CARE FOR FLASHBACKS/TRIGGERS

Pray for the comfort of the Holy Spirit.

Acknowledge that you are having a flashback and remind yourself that it is not the actual event.

Breathe slowly, take deep breaths. This is important because when we panic, our body begins to take short, shallow breaths and the decrease in oxygen that accompanies this change can increase our panicked state. Increasing the oxygen in your system will help you calm down. Get a drink of water to make sure you are well hydrated, which helps your brain rebound.

Return to the present. Take time to establish where you are in the present. Look around you and take note of the colors in the room. Listen to the sounds that are happening around you. Smell the scents that are in the room with you. Feel the clothes on your skin and take note of the different parts of your body (hands, feet, etc.)

When you are ready, take some time to think about the trigger of your automatic reaction. Determine if there is some way you could alter the situation so that the trigger does not happen or does not affect you in the same way. For example, perhaps changing the setup of the room would be helpful, or asking your partner not to do the activity that you believe may have set off your flashback.

If you are being triggered while being intimate with a partner, discuss with your partner what you would like her/him to do when you have an automatic reaction (e.g. stop what they are doing, hold you, talk to you, sit with you, etc.) Ask your partner to watch for signs that you are having an automatic reaction, and to stop sexual activity immediately when you have one.

> What changes can you make to the sights, sounds, smell, and feel of your room to make it a safer and more loving environment for you and your spouse? _____
> _____
> _____
> _____
> _____
> _____
> _____
> _____
> _____
> _____

Recognize what would make you feel safer. Wrap yourself in a blanket; shut yourself in a room; pray...whatever it takes to feel secure. Share your feelings with someone you trust and understand that you aren't crazy or doing something wrong; you just need to allow yourself time to heal.

> I feel safe and secure when I... _____
> _____
> _____
> _____
> _____
> _____
> _____

What are some ways in which you can show love for your spouse other than the physical act of sex itself? _____

_____
_____
_____
_____
_____
_____
_____
_____

Taking a break from sexual activity is essential at some point in the healing journey. Even after marriage, there may be times when you need time to consider your own sexual self without worrying about someone else's needs. By eliminating sex from the picture, you have the freedom to work on transparency and building a trusting relationship in safety. Feeling cherished and respected is important to a survivor. This becomes essential as friendships turn to romance, and romance turns into a deeper, more intimate sexual relationship.

SENSUALITY EXERCISE:

In this exercise concerning sensuality, your partner will give you a massage without culminating in intercourse. This is a time for you to reflect on what triggers flashbacks for you as you set up the room. Eliminate those sights, sounds, smells, and textures that may trigger you. Add to the room ones that make you feel calm, comfortable, and content. Find a fragrance that takes you to a happy place. Find a texture of bedding that makes you feel good. You may want soft, romantic music or none at all.

Once the room has been prepared, lay under a sheet. Your partner should expose one part of your body at a time and rub lotion on you. Voice your thoughts and feelings. Inform your partner of what feels good and any movement, touch, smell, or sound which makes you uneasy. Your partner should be observant of your body language and respond positively to your comments.

End the massage without the compulsion to perform—no sex and no reciprocation at this time. Instead hold one another and talk and /or sleep. Later you can discuss possible reciprocation of this experience.

Describe how this exercise made you feel. _____
_____
_____
_____
_____

SEXUAL ATTITUDES

*This chart comes from The Sexual Healing Journey by Wendy Maltz

Sexual Attitudes	
Sexual Abuse Mind-set (sex = sexual abuse)	Healthy Sexual Attitudes (sex = positive sexual energy)
Sex is uncontrollable energy	Sex is controllable energy
Sex is an obligation	Sex is a choice
Sex is addictive	Sex is a natural drive
Sex is hurtful	Sex is nurturing, healing
Sex is a condition for receiving love	Sex is an expression of love
Sex is "doing to" someone	Sex is sharing with someone
Sex is a commodity	Sex is part of who I am
Sex is void of communication	Sex requires communication
Sex is secretive	Sex is private
Sex is exploitive	Sex is respectful
Sex is deceitful	Sex is honest
Sex benefits one person	Sex is mutual
Sex is emotionally distant	Sex is intimate
Sex is irresponsible	Sex is responsible
Sex is unsafe	Sex is safe
Sex has no limits	Sex has boundaries
Sex is power over someone	Sex is empowering

EXERCISE:

Mark the boxes that apply to your thoughts about sex. Discuss your thoughts and feelings with your spouse and/or your counselor to develop healthy attitudes.

_____
_____
_____
_____
_____
_____

Determining healthy attitudes and behaviors about sex can offer tremendous peace to the survivor. It removes some of the fears you may have about what is expected as part of a loving sexual relationship.

EXERCISE:

Pray alone and with your spouse for the courage and the words to discuss your physical intimacy needs. Schedule a time when you will be uninterrupted and a location in which you are comfortable. Take turns voicing your needs without interruption. Explain what needs are currently being met and which ones need improvement. Be prepared to offer suggestions for meeting those needs. Please write these down. _____
_____
_____
_____
_____
_____
_____

Review the following True Intimacy contract with your spouse and discuss its implications. Discuss your thoughts about these terms and what it would mean to you. Consider it a sacred covenant between the two of you. Place it with your other important documents or frame it and hang it in your bedroom.

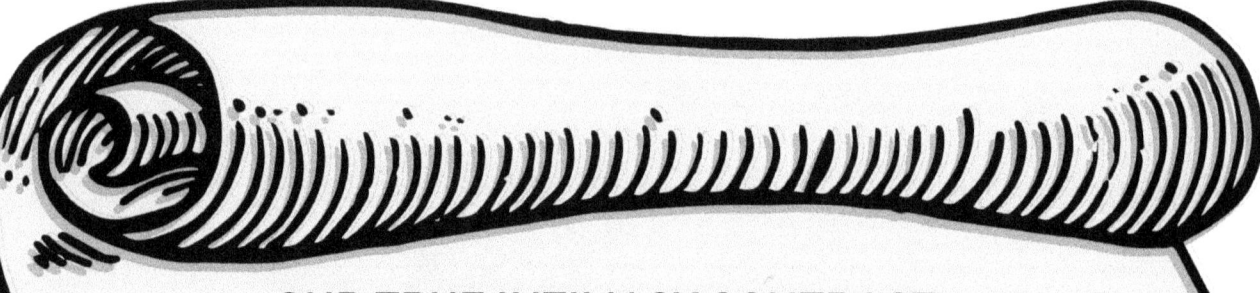

OUR TRUE INTIMACY CONTRACT

Out of mutual love and respect, we agree to this contract as part of a healthy and safe intimate relationship with our soul mate.

- It is okay to say no to sex or any sexual act at ANY TIME.
- We can voice how we are feeling or what we need at ANY TIME.
- We don't ever have to perform sexually in any manner we feel uncomfortable.
- We will take a break or stop sexual activity whenever either of us requests it.
- It's okay to ask for what we want sexually, without being teased or shamed for doing so.
- We don't have to disclose the details of a previous sexual relationship unless that information is important to our sexual relationship or our partner's physical health.
- Our sexual thoughts and fantasies are our own, and we don't have to share them with each other unless we choose.
- We can initiate or decline sex without incurring a negative reaction from our partner.
- Sex will not be used as a weapon or expected as a reward.
- We will abide by the agreement we have pertaining to birth control or family planning.
- We agree to be responsive to each other's needs in matters of physical comfort.
- What we do sexually is private and not to be discussed with others outside our relationship unless necessary for medical or mental health treatment.
- We will not view or read pornography.
- We are ultimately responsible for our own sexual fulfillment by expressing our needs.
- We will actively listen to and respond to the sexual needs of our partner.
- We will not have any romantic or sexual interactions with any other person, including phone or cyber affairs.
- We realize sex is a sacred gift from God and will treat it accordingly.

Other:_____

Husband _____ Wife _____ Date _____

Consequences*: _____

*Once you and your partner have agreed on your complete set of guidelines in your sexual relationship, you should also discuss what the potential consequences will be for breaking one of the guidelines.

Be patient. As time passes and you experience positive sexual experiences, you will naturally move towards more healthy sexual attitudes. The sacred bond between you will grow and you can enjoy a satisfying and rewarding love life as God intended for you from the beginning.

CONCLUSION

True intimacy is like a river flowing through our lives bringing us joy, and like water, giving the much needed nutrients to relationships to help them grow and prosper. As survivors, we tend to build dams to hold back that flow, which limits our ability to love and be loved. We have great empathy for the abuse you have suffered and the residual impact of that abuse on your capacity to open yourself up to possible hurt.

Unfortunately, in this life there are always going to be disappointments in relationships, but we must focus on the overwhelming satisfaction that true intimacy can bring into our lives. We encourage you to be intentional about sharing more of yourself with others and allowing them to get closer. We also encourage you to take an inventory of your relationships and apply the principles you have learned in this study to enrich your connections with God, others and your intimate partner.

God bless you on this pathway to healing from past hurts to rewarding intimate relationships.

ANGELA'S VOICE

Angela's Voice is dedicated to developing, distributing, and endorsing valuable resources in the awareness, prevention, and healing of child sexual abuse. The materials, though specific for survivors of child sexual abuse, also benefit any abuse survivor and help protect children by teaching them how to defend themselves from abusive behavior. Founder Angela Williams, MFP, is a survivor-turned-advocate who shares a powerful message of triumph over tragedy by sharing her vulnerable and candid voice about her abuse trauma, her pain, her struggles, and her journey to healing in hopes that it may help other survivors expedite their healing journey.

Williams has devoted years to providing awareness, prevention, and healing programs through her advocacy work. Williams has captivated audiences with her powerful message of triumph over tragedy as a victim of childhood physical and sexual abuse. At age seventeen, she attempted suicide, and that day was the end of her torment and the beginning of a journey to healing. She is a crusader for change and dedicates her life to eradicate child sexual abuse. She holds a master's in forensic psychology with a concentration in child abuse. Williams is a powerful messenger, appearing in national and international news and documentaries. She has been successful in state legislative reform and national policy work and served on the Policy Committee of the National Coalition to Prevent Child Sexual Abuse and Exploitation. She has received numerous accolades and awards for her work, including her collection of books that have valuable lessons for survivors of all ages.

Please follow Angela Williams on social media and contact angelasvoice.com to book a speaking event or interview.

Books by Angela Williams

Loving Me: After Abuse
From Sorrows to Sapphires, Angela Williams's Memoir

Interactive Workbooks—Adults

Healing
Pathway to Healing, Guide to Healing
True Intimacy
Shattering the Shame
Unveiling Child Sexual Abuse

Prevention
Tough Talk to Tender Hearts
The Grooming Mystery
Single Parenting Solutions
Courage to Speak

Children's Books (Ages 5–10)
Gracie Finds Her Voice
Grant Gets His Shield
Gracie and Grant's Big Win
Gracie and Grant's Big Win Coloring Book
Find Your Voice Curriculum Book

Join the Angela's Voice Movement

Take action to break the silence and cycle of Child Sexual Abuse and Exploitation

HELP US SAVE THE NEXT GENERATION OF CHILDREN!

1. Be a Child Advocate
2. Donate at angelasvoice.com
3. Invite Angela Williams to Speak
4. Purchase another Angela's Voice Prevention or Healing Book

Discover more child sexual abuse prevention and healing resources at angelasvoice.com and follow angelasvoice in social media.

Instagram @Angelasvoice

Facebook @Angelasvoice

Twitter @Angelasvoice

Linkedin/angelasvoice

Angelasvoice.blogspot.com

Youtube.com/angelakwilliams

www.ingramcontent.com/pod-product-compliance
Lightning Source LLC
Chambersburg PA
CBHW040010080526
44586CB00028B/2952